DOOMSTEAD DAYS

ALSO BY BRIAN TEARE

BOOKS

The Room Where I Was Born

Pleasure

Sight Map

Companion Grasses

The Empty Form Goes All the Way to Heaven

CHAPBOOKS

Pilgrim

Transcendental Grammar Crown

↑

Paradise Was Typeset

Helplessness

[black sun crown]

SORE EROS

Headlands Quadrats

DOOMSTEAD DAYS

BRIAN TEARE

NIGHTBOAT BOOKS

NEW YORK

ISBN: 978-1-64362-002-2

Design and typesetting by Janet Evans-Scanlon
Text set in Garamond and Alternate Gothic
Cover design: Mary Austin Speaker
Cover Art: "Water" by David Wojnarowicz, 1987
Courtesy of the Estate of David Wojnarowicz and
P•P•O•W, New York. © David Wojnarowicz.

Cataloging-in-publication data is available from
the Library of Congress

Nightboat Books
New York
www.nightboat.org

Our contemporary concern with World Order
seems specially charged with a crisis in language
and world; we are in apocalyptic times. But . . .
the feeling of coming to the end or the beginning
of things never comes to an end & is always
a beginning.

ROBERT DUNCAN
"Man's Fulfillment in Order & Strife"

To praise this, blame that,
Leads one subtly away from the beginning, where
We must stay, in motion.

JOHN ASHBERY
Houseboat Days

In a global state of precarity, we don't have
choices other than looking for life in this ruin.

ANNA LOWENHAUPT TSING
The Mushroom at the End of the World

The day's all description and what is he now?

REGINALD SHEPHERD
Angel, Interrupted

CONTENTS

CLEAR WATER RENGA

fog, error, radar
  failed :: the container ship hit
    the bridge tower hard ::

    its hull split, spilled fifty eight
     thousand gallons of bunker

         fuel oil :: November
     7th, 2007 ::
    the next day it hurt

    the eyes to walk dockside, wind
   bringing the sting of petrol ::

each of its pilings
  ringed with rainbow, from the pier
   I watched white boats go

    trailing bright yellow booms, saw
    how the real absorbs a fact

                              the way a seabird
                      preens its greased wings helplessly,
            the ordinary

                gesture gently carrying
        toxins from feather to beak,

from outside to in ::
            it was the first disaster
                    I could walk to, look

                    at until it ceased to seem
                            exceptional, no matter

                                    the panic I felt
                            watching an oiled Western grebe
                    thrash against capture,

                no matter the bird slipping
        in the clear plastic tub slicked

by its own feathers,
            its rescuer trying to
                    contain it without

                    injury :: easier to
                        watch rescuers soak the bird

                                    in warm water, Dawn
                          dish soap :: easier to watch
                  them scrape each feather

                  clean with a kids' toothbrush :: but
        I couldn't get over it,

how the real couldn't
        refuse, could do nothing but
                disburse tar ball, sheen,

                        & slick from the central Bay
                                on currents west through the Gate

                                        until the whole coast,
                                Marin to Pacifica
                        to the Farallones,

                        absorbed the new fact the real
        had given it :: & didn't

each image likewise
        sink into my mind's archive
                of the disaster,

                        each stashed fact evidence of
                                an attachment to events

                                        I neither forget
                              nor understand :: for three years
                        I've kept newspaper

                        clippings & old emails, kept
              the photo of an oiled surf

scoter in the hands
          of a panicked passersby,
                    Megan McNertny,

                    who tried, untrained, to save it
                              barehanded, its smeared feathers

                                             as flat black & wet
                              as its eye eying the lens ::
                        I've kept some numbers ::

                    seven thousand birds dead, two
              hundred miles of coast coated,

forty four point four
          million dollars paid by Fleet
                    Management, owners

                    of the Cosco-Busan wreck ::
                        I've kept track of herring spawn

                    exposed to fuel oil,
              how sunlight creates photo-
        toxic conditions

              crippling embryonic fish,
        how herring won't return to

seasonal breeding
        grounds polluted by the spill ::
              & I've kept track of

              other disasters that came
                    up close :: in 2008

                          the Summit Fire
                    in the Santa Cruz Mountains
              consumed four thousand

              acres in six days in May,
        & the next year in August

the Lockheed Fire burned
        nearly eight thousand acres
              in eleven days ::

              a tarry charred horizon
                    drew the sun down, blunted light

fat with ash that stuck
to our window sills :: each day
a weird hot wind left

evidence of how crisis
becomes most real through firsthand

fact :: the war'd been on
all those years but not so close
I could walk to it,

its smoke staining my snot black,
meaning, I think, the local

real made me begin
to experience the mind
as a form porous

as mile after mile of trees
accepting fire, to begin

to see aftermath
as the start of thought, the way
some conifers need

extreme heat to unseal seeds
locked in the resinous bracts

                              of cones :: Monterey,
                    Knobcone, & Bishop pines, born
              natives of flame :: but

                 I couldn't get over it,
         the endless capacity

of the real for fact,
         how it seems to have at core
                 endless hollowness

                    my mind can never mimic
                       given its capacity

                                    for reaction, how
                       the real will accept any
                  thing, but when I looked

                 up at the drift of cinders
         & soot that settled a singe

in the trees, I knew
         I was afraid :: a raptor's
                 accurate shadow

                    falling over me always
                       premonitory, I go

                              north to Marin, miles
                       from any city limit,
                  to land protected

                       by law, to walk, to outpace
            panic as if my mind could

give like the long lines
            of wire fence that guide the drive
                  to Tomales Point ::

                       Pierce Point Road rides out over
                              hills dry in July :: high fire

                                          danger day, grasses
                              a gold nerve pricked by thistle ::
                       though "scenic views" line

                       the road, the surround is sky
            without horizon, silver

vague sun haze :: vision's
            discursive limit :: mostly
                  I want to live there,

                       the precise site the mind stops
                              its blameless languaging job ::

as if there the real
stops burning, oil its gush from
the uncapped well :: no ::

it's July 2010 ::
I've spent weeks watching YouTube

footage of a flight
over BP's Deepwater
Horizon oil spill ::

John L. Wathen, Tom Hutchins,
& David Helvarg took off

on June 25th
from Gulf Shores, Alabama,
five hours due south of

my hometown :: "It didn't take
long to find our first oil. In

the mouth of Mobile
Bay there were scattered patches
of light sheen behind

the islands," Dauphin Island
the one I know from summer

                                        roadtrips years before
                              Gulf barrier islands lost
                    landmass & wildlife

                              habitat to Katrina ::
                    footage shows just "One point two

miles off Gulf Shores there
          was a solid mass of oil.
                    On previous flights

                    behind Petit Bois Island,
                              all we'd seen was light sheen—now

                                                  it was turning to
                                        darker pink mats, some miles long
                              & hundreds of feet

                    wide." :: all day as I walk out
          to Tomales Point & back

the soft warm water
          distant in crisis churns, turns
                    the Pacific strange ::

                    a high white sun blanks the waves
                              whitecaps shatter with spindrift

                      & the burning Gulf
                keeps burning, water on fire
          the purest endgame,

             obvious allegory
       like some Revelations plague,

chapter eight verse ten ::
      after the first & second
          angels, what soul could

           watch the third bear its trumpet
            & not fear the imminent

                        music, the song meant
                  to call a star down to earth
              to fall bitterness

           "on a third of the rivers
        & the springs of the waters"

& turn the waters
      to wormwood :: I ask you :: who
          could watch & forget

         the sour wells & fallow
           fields that follow industry

where it follows us ::
I walk north & find lupine
opening its sweet

furred purse of bees :: to the east
where gusts rip through Windy Gap,

hawks, wings rigid, ride
zephyrs so fierce it takes strength
to go nowhere :: here

the cobweb thistle's winding
a bobbin's worth of white silk

through white-tipped spikes :: but
I can't forget to rewind
the crisis, to pause

the footage where the plane spots
a pod of dolphins, their fins

streaked with sheen :: I can't
forget Coast Guard planes have been
sent over the coast

at night to spray Corexit,
a dispersant BP said

                              would ease the cleanup
                        but instead bonds with the oil
                  to create toxins

              that move through skin & rupture
        red blood cells, toxins that cause

internal bleeding
            & indefinite headaches
                        in oil cleanup crews

                  & folks living near the spill   ::
                        it even disrupts the life

                                    cycles of marine
                              animals by dispersing
                        the lipids in sperm,

                  the toxins piggybacking
        on reproduction to turn

life against itself ::
        I can't forget how we've made
                  a poison nature's

                  second nature, how the real
                        seems dependent on this fact ::

                              everywhere we live
                    we destroy life :: I could walk
              due north all my years

                    & never not stand the way
        I stand on land Coast Miwok

once camped on to fish
        peak salmon runs :: seasonal,
                cyclical, the tribe

                    for centuries walked to shore
                        then walked back inland to hunt

                                    Mule deer, centuries
                              following sustenance through
                    landscape :: settlers

                    uncalendared that walking
        ritual, the hunt's sacred

to-&-fro :: after
        displacement, European
                disease, slavery,

                    & assimilation, few
                        members of the tribe survived

by 1880
when Pierce Point Ranch raised cattle
for butter & cheese

sold south to San Francisco ::
it challenges the white mind

to look at this coast
& think *this is a ruin* ::
yellow bush lupine

grows so thick I have to push
through it toward the Pacific

light unfolding, flexed
open like a gold poppy ::
the Pierce family ranched

until forty years ago,
after dairy cows raised on

European feed
grass extirpated native
coastal prairie plants

& the Tule elk who fed
on them :: after the ranch closed,

                                        its white barn quiet,
                                the point became national
                        seashore ::   a mile north

                        of the Upper Ranch, our long
                fraught occupation flowers

non-native clover
        & rye grazed off-trail by elk
                calves & their mothers,

                part of a four-hundred head
                        herd whose progenitors were

                                        brought back to the Point
                                in the Seventies, a herd
                        monitored year-round

                by park rangers housed on this
        land once traveled by Miwok

whose descendants live
        inland with Southern Pomo
                on land the tribes, now

                Federated Indians
                        of Graton Rancheria,

                                        bought & put in trust ::
                              life, habitat, & ruin
                    run recombinant

                         & helical in hurt forms
              that keep life going & do

not heal, its pattern
          the gist of a missive sent
                    by my friend Martha,

                         southern Louisiana,
                              June 10th :: "After some time home,

                                        it's clear—the drilling
                              moratorium's no good.
                    The economy

                    will collapse, stranding people
          & undercutting support

for alternative
          energy research. Nothing
                    moves forward as long

                         as green energy & oil
                              are antagonists. These folks

have worked to feed us
for years. To abandon them
is not right." :: for years

I've walked as far as it takes
to walk past thought into what

might be called image,
        non-discursive :: I spend hours
            so empty my mind's

        the ranch barn open both ends
            to wind, nothing but old hay

                                stirring in the stalls ::
                    it used to seem indulgent
                to vanish outward

            into the texture of elk
        fur on the hills of White Gulch,

its two-toned velvet
        gold then brown against brighter
                brittle grasses, but

            even then I still dwell in
                the real, our occupation,

                              the American
                        goldfinch husking invasive
                  thistle seed for feed

                  the large paradox writ small ::
            each image that replaces

consciousness *is*
            the real, as temporary
                  as any desire

                  to do no harm here, the mind
                        a Bishop pine splayed by wind

                                    during its long wait
                              for fire, local to this
                        coast & a native

                  of the phenomenal world ::
            toward sunset, I stop, sit

at the lower Ranch
            pond, its worn shore scored with sedge
                  & the hooves of elk ::

                  in such late light its surface
                        relaxes, pure reflection ::

                    I look :: an elk steps
              forward from the sedge :: it steps
        into the image

              of an elk who steps forward
        from the sedge & bends its head

to drink from my mouth ::
        & bends & from my mouth drinks
              clear water ::

                              for Brenda Hillman & Martha Serpas

HEADLANDS QUADRATS

past the decommissioned fort
past the former nike missile site

past the abandoned battery
past the empty gun platform

past dugouts lined with concrete
sandbags
                    the ocean

Pacific fog channels
through the Golden Gate

cliffside where gulls steer
into sheer hovering

wind shakes a single branch
of sticky monkey flower

ridge top the path forks
up further to fog or down

to steep crowded terraced
clarity lupine & thistle

oystercatchers & black
sand tide coats with foam

the trail's last ten feet
crumble & run to sand

slant stairs end mid-air
above beach why wait

to turn this distance
to metaphor
                    just jump

off the ridge above
a tourist pisses a relief

to be in a landscape
where purity isn't possible

sacred profane a pain
in the ass mostly

the mind wants to be
red-tailed way up there

hanging out in the wind
not worrying about the fate

of nature the coyote shits
on the road to mark it

like an animal in its habitat
an idea needs room to move

within its preferred range
like the rufous-sided towhee

in its spangled black cape
rattling chaparral along the trail

only sometimes
an idea lets itself

be seen singing
buzzy *tea* buzzy *tea*

to think I have to
walk around looking

a young copse slanting
up to the ridge sends up

a spiral of insects
around a centripetal axis

the flycatchers also swing
out from & return to

chasing prey a kind
of looping beauty

off-kilter wobbling
like a saucer toward

stasis for an hour
I watch it not stop

maybe a mind sated
with image won't move

the raccoon must have
eaten snails for a half-mile

trail littered with shells
stripped brittle old tin

I don't know the rules
but I follow them

downhill into extravagant
thistle from which a doe

startles a spark struck
from flint fear mostly

faster than predators
on the trail I encounter

for the first time a coyote
exactly the color of July

in these hills unhurried
it turns to me full of bones

home's an angle
I follow down trail

long grass under
foot worn short

burnished bronze
coarse horse hair

a big eucalyptus downed
the power line & brings

flame to bracken the deer
leap out of into the field

past houses people emerge
from thinking *smoke I smell*

smoke fire by then louder
than the coming sirens

eucalyptus non-native
invasive flammable

camouflage the army
planted to hide the fort

military housing
designed to fold

the soldiers' bodies
into the landscape

pastures shorn
by horses grazing

each evening the houses
lean shadow against

the ridge we curl into
during a different war

without trees to shade
their names soldiers did too

ocean on the other side
of our sleep all the plump

pearly everlasting means
wildflower season isn't over

though it's late summer
grasses reseeding already

down from the ridge
fallen seeds follow

my wake far as the trail
behind the old barn

where coyotes leave
scat full of fur & forage

fit occasion to say
a litany of their names

dogtail foxtail
beard barley rye

a list of ships on which
the season sails home

In Memoriam
Joanne Kyger, 1934-2017

TOXICS RELEASE INVENTORY
(*Essay on Man*)

the quick hard quake slaps
          the building as I unpack ::
   5.8, handfuls

                        of plaster scattered
                like salt on the dark wood floors
                       I buy a new broom

to sweep :: my first day
          in Philadelphia feels
   like San Francisco,

                   the tectonic earth
        alert here too :: it's my self-
                      same self feels newly

estranged the way books
          I put in the same order
   back on the shelves look

different :: I open
the new notebook on a walk
later that same day

outside the Woodlands
Cemetery, the struck deer
a dark startle, white

underside stained, tail
still raised in escape :: I write
how breeze stirs its fur,

seems like shallow breath,
& a passing car flattens
the arched cardboard, box

springing back after
so it seems an animal
on its side again,

its breath just some wind
lifting paper skin, the white
plastic bag I thought

43

                                   was its signature
              undercolor :: heat ripples
                                             the distance I walk

over Chester Ave. ::
              I write I think four dogs run
         across the red brick

                                   building abandoned
                   like the lot it sits next to,
                                        pack of wheat-pasted

paper dogs unleashed
              in a field green as August
         gets here, bull thistle

                                   taller than stalks of
                   timothy inflorescing,
                                        fringing the sidewalk ::

the notebook keeps it
              alive, my first month out east
         when I miss so much

                              the hills of Marin
                    Headlands my mind contrives lives
                                        from paper, the twinned

images of doe
                    & dogs a crest I carry
            out onto the streets

                                        of my new city
                        as a kind of irony,
                                        a bestiary

alienated
                        from actual animals
            the way coming east

                                        announces itself
                    as a way of life :: goodbye
                                        summer grass the same

lean dry rough color
                    of the golden coyote
            hunting, goodbye ridge

                high behind the house
        & the spotted owl who leaves
                      bony pellets there

on the trail beneath
        its nest in the old live oak ::
    I write it all down

                & try to move on,
       walk through one eastern season
                  into another,

not realizing
       the city's marketplace makes
    itself seem a vast

              panorama, each
      image reduced & distant
               with the illusion

of depth it offers
       as currency :: the city
    conducts its business

                                        trading the wishes
                    of citizens for empty
                                                    actuality

we walk out into,
                    the future a proffered naught
              beneath our feet, sealed

                                        soil infertile, streets
                    & sidewalks yielding nothing
                                                but surface runoff

polluted with oil,
                    gasoline, antifreeze, trash
              washed from gutters to

                                        sewers to rivers
                    by heavy rains :: all summer
                                                we walk on pavement

that radiates heat
                    long after midnight :: I wait
              for the 40 bus

near a red brick wall
& feel it seethe like sunburn
under a t-shirt ::

while I wait I write
what I've learned about August
in the city, write

urban heat island
& *the albedo quotient*
of sun-struck structures

painted white, then stop
when the paper, wicking sweat
from my palm, tears :: next

there are months I write
nothing while my life goes on
as historical

& ordinary
in its muteness as any
street full of cars parked

                              before the morning
          commute :: sometimes the image
                                            of empty cars feels

eerie, its false calm
              a sort of memorial
          to wars fought off shore,

                                      sometimes the image
                      seems like the first frames of film
                                            before the horror

begins to arrive,
                & then my neighbor waves hi
          as he walks his kids

                                      to school & they seem
                      exempt from the drone warfare
                                            from which we are not

exempted, our lives
                a vast elaborate set
          behind whose facade

                                                                          49

                              the state hopes to hide
              from public view the human
                                        cost of war, a shame

everything's stained by
                after a long cold winter,
          its dirty drifts cloaked

                                      in new snow   :: outside
                    a sharp metal edge scrapes ice
                                          off sidewalk, grating

that grieves the back teeth
                  until I can taste the sound,
            bitter & sour ::

                                        it comes off in scraps,
                  orts, & fragments, in layers,
                                          the civilian

experience in
              America :: beneath lies
          a surface the mind

                                    strikes, thinking into
                    ink the way ink thinks into
                                                paper :: all the walls,

the protecting walls
                    & the reflecting walls, wear
            so terribly thin

                                    in this war, writes Woolf
                    in her notebook on Wednesday
                                    July 24th,

1940 :: while
                    I was writing, a bomb dropped
            so close the pen jumped

                                    out of my fingers,
                    she notes late that September,
                                    & what is war now

that Spruce Street's quiet,
                    my black shoes rimed white by salt
            as I walk, reading

                    the city image
          by image, its surfaces
                              hinting at a life

fugitive, hidden ::
                    I stop at the flower stand ::
          tulips in buckets ::

                              a small dog begging
          to be picked up, passersby
                              telling the woman

walking the dog *rock*
                    salt is sharp & hurts its paws,
          & the woman flat

                                        out ignoring them,
                    her dog limping by lilies,
                                        early daffodils,

irises, & long
                    branches of pussy willow,
          each catkin a node

                                        of snow :: late empire
                        at work in the images
                                                pouring in, *FRESH CUT*

FLOWERS flowering
                runoff & pesticides, sprayed
        day laborers sick

                                        from the exposure,
                        thousands of pounds of carbon
                                                pumped from planes & trucks

refrigerated
                to get beauty here unharmed ::
        I stand back to look

                                        at the white lily,
                        at its dramatic anthers,
                                                how orange dark pollen,

large-grained, falls, stipples
                its waxy petals with stain,
        & think the city

                                    has a similar
                        beauty :: both figure & ground
                                                vanish in a plane

of shapes, the buildings
                    distilled by snow down to white
            exaggerated

                                            geometry, life
                            abstracted, linked by the new
                                                    materials fused

to being :: curbside
                    ice made frangible by thaw
            does this antique lace

                                            thing at its edges
                            black as a handkerchief dragged
                                                    through car oil & ash,

its saturated
                    fabric disclosing trash :: cups,
            plastic bottle caps,

Styrofoam peanuts,
cigarette butts, each cast-off
polymer a link

in an industry
chain fabricated to last,
extending far as

creation's ample
range extends :: the scale of
sensual, mental

pow'rs ascends ::
& mark how it mounts, to man's
imperial race

from green myriads
in the peopled grass, writes Pope
in *Essay on Man* ::

so I stand & look
at the white lily, the white
city, its surface

of commodities
an immense pretense :: beneath,
a thousand trade routes

run rough parallel
to thought & I follow them
out into the words

I touch through rhythm,
notebook open as I walk,
stride inflecting script

with wobble & slant,
blots & warps made by sweat, all
the raw errata

of the transcribing
body :: images follow
a logic I see

I can hear, my ear
an eye in dilation :: there
the city's center

seizes my senses
with noise total as weather ::
gate slam, garbage can,

bus brakes, a waitress
complaining on her smoke break,
two small shrill dogs thrilled

into conniptions
in the pet shop's front window,
four listing frat boys

laughing as they piss
in the bar's back parking lot ::
in spring, beneath trees

helplessly budding
during days of freezing rain,
past flowers & spires,

after my landlord
cheats the lease by replacing
the radiators

with electric heat
so weak all winter I can't
afford to live in

more than one warm room,
I walk out as if to make
peace with the city,

its coercive hurt,
to face the weird sure feeling
of being alive

& always under-
mined, unsure if suspicion
& resistance will

just undermine me
further with exemplary
bad faith :: I walk out

into late empire
as if walking could conjure
a calming charm, *charm*

                                     from *carmen*, Latin

                      for *song* :: but O I am so

                                              easy to distract ::

a handsome man keeps

                  saying my name, *Oh Brian*,

            an experience

                                     all apostrophe

                      & lubrication until

                                  he pulls out, condom

broken :: so I bend

                  over the metal table,

            so I say *Ah*, so

                                  the nurse stabs my ass

                      & throat with swabs & orders

                                      a urine sample,

blood draw, & rapid

                  HIV test :: possibly

            infected, I roll

                                          my sleeve, make a fist
                    a biohazard, & leave
                                                    to piss in a cup

& give a survey
                    numbers that turn libido
          to mere statistics ::

                                                    for fifteen minutes
                    I sit, waiting for results,
                                          & feel the plastic

impersonal chair
                    go all eidetic :: panicked
          once we'd wait for weeks

                                          to get the dreaded
                    clinic call, impossible
                                          weeks spent replaying

each sexual act ::
                    not out of lust :: out of fear,
          obsessing over

risks taken, the threat
always present :: medicine
able to offer

then only knowing
your status & little else ::
negative, she says,

but still at risk :: so
the clinician prescribes three
pricey pills daily

for a month, a post-
exposure prophylaxis
system that will kill

virus too latent
to be detected early ::
I puke for a week,

am not infected,
& this is progress I go
out into, open

                              to the storm I pause
              under an awning to watch ::
                                        wind gusts a dozen

small black umbrellas
                    inside out :: a Hokusai
              rain so straight & thin

                                        it comes in pitched at
                    an angle steep to people
                                        on the streets, their shirts

soaked :: after it stops
                    I write I walk among trees
              next to a tall man

                                        they resemble more
                    for a distant trembling
                                        sweetness in his mien

than his slender height,
                    & the Wissahickon twists
              frigid, diminished

                              through mud the cliffs jut
                above, famous schist that breaks
                                        off itself in sheets ::

now clear isinglass,
                now pearly abalone ::
        & is fragile, prone

                                        to fracture, to flakes
                        that lend dirt its signature
                                                shimmer :: we walk hills

high above the creek
                & startle a fox whose run
        hurts the forest hush

                                with the sudden crash
                of bracken & leaf litter,
                                        each leap amplified

in the echoing
                empty branches :: I stand there
        beside the tall man

                              in silence the fox
              leaves behind, & want to stay,
                                        black shoes glittering

with schist, all the noise
                of the city not equal
        to the animal

                                        improbable there
                among us :: I try to write
                                        it down :: the image

resists transcription
                the way the fox insists on
        its distance from us ::

                                        my mind keeps striking
                against its surface as if
                                        it were hard, urban,

scraping its red coat
                down to the city hidden
        inside the living

                              animal, organs
                    heavy with the lead thirty
                                        six smelters left north

in the Delaware
                    River Wards, anatomy
            a map of grids skewed

                                      by diagonals
                    & two sinuous rivers,
                                        contaminated

map of pipes & tracks
                    that truck crude from the west to
            the refinery

                                      in Point Breeze, a map
                    of black paws I dream I hold
                                        to make sure I hit

the white gut I split
                    open in augury :: out
            of the clean cut spills

                         over three hundred
             thousand pounds of sulfuric
                                   acid, one hundred

fifty four thousand
             of hydrogen cyanide,
        twenty eight thousand

                              of cumene, toxics
             released onsite, byproducts
                                   of refining crude

chuted through wetlands
             off the river, the Schuylkill
        too a casualty

                              of Pennsylvania
             trade since 1866,
                                   when secure passage

to the Atlantic
             meant the first refinery
        bought farmland & built

on the riverbank ::
I dream again I exhaust
                              the fox I chase deep

in snow in the hills
                above the Wissahickon,
        & find it dead, curled

                                in upon itself ::
                this time its slit skin reveals
                                a little hellscape,

its interior
                some kind of diorama ::
        a sunken oil barge

                                surges crude, a slick
                igniting the way it did
                                in the Seventies ::

the river's surface
                gathers in a writhe of smoke,
        & all of it :: oil,

fire, water, ash :: pours
out of the fox whose body
shrivels, shivering,

issuing toxics
that hiss as they hit the snow,
the city finished

with hiding itself
in skin :: each fox I dream dies
with didactic poise,

& I write them down
sheepishly, their obvious
allegorical

ends, among the nonce
system of rhymes, images,
phrases, quotations,

rhythms, facts, & scrawls,
lines that link or cross them out ::
the notebook's open,

                                        additive, a choice
                        situation for desire's
                                                greedy accretive

& / & / & / & / &
                        endlessly :: see :: through this air,
                this ocean, this earth,

                                        all matter quick, burst-
                        ing into birth :: how high life
                                                may go! how wide! how

deep extend below!
                writes Pope, & I hear instead
        of his praise the change

                                        we bring to the terms
                        of life, how we make matter
                                        an antagonist

when industry goes
                so wide, so deep, & touches
        us so totally

we find our final
privacies violated ::
benzene & styrene,

toluene & n-
hexane, carbon disulfide
& acetone :: six

toxics present in
ninety four to one hundred
percent of people

tested, both urban
& rural, people whose blood
& urine carries

the cost of merely
breathing as they go to work ::
& are not broken

by contaminants,
or are not yet broken by
the slow violence

                                        latent in the wake
                        of bioaccumulants
                                                    & synergistic

toxins stored in fat,
                    in the liver & kidneys
                where one errancy

                                        can birth an illness
                        that quickens matter the way
                                                the refinery

visits affliction
                    upon working class neighbors
                through onsite toxics

                                        released into air ::
                        breathing sulfuric acid
                                                fumes leads to asthma

the way benzene gas
                    fosters cognitive problems
                & leukemia

in extreme cases ::
it's so bad, having these fumes
in your mouth, & not

knowing what they are,
says activist Teresa
Hill, who lives nearby

with her kids who can't
breathe without medical bills
totaling thousands ::

I write down *asthma*
cluster, environmental
racism, under-

line her words, then
a line of Merleau-Ponty's ::
where are we to put

the limit between
the body & the world, since
all the world is flesh? ::

                                    the question's stakes change
                        when I think of tasting fumes
                                        as I mouth the words ::

some marry the world
                I write next in the notebook
            & I don't know what

                                    I mean by *marry*
                        or *world* :: what is the feeling
                                        that sends me walking

out of my childhood
                into the pines behind it
            until grass rises

                                    above my head, field
                        a world more of things than facts,
                                        & sunset touches

the ceiling of seeds
                I hide under :: what is it
            I feel as I walk

back to the tight knot
each night ties around the house ::
let the image be

my answer, I write,
let the image answer me ::
when I clear the pines

I stand just outside
the scant light the house casts off ::
its steady edge *is*

the limit between
my body's flesh & the world's ::
the limit is learned

& gender teaches
us where to put it if race
doesn't :: white queer boy,

I marry the world
because, as a child pressing
against it, I feel

no limits to flesh,
just the crush of pine needles
& sticky resin,

the white commonplace
of feeling safe I seek out
when safety fails me

inside :: even then
I can accept the violence
that arises from

being a mammal,
our bloody given bodies
of glands & hormones,

our lust & fucking,
the ways we change as we age
& die :: but I hate

what happens inside
the house, the hierarchies
& made fake limits

               of family life
        enforced by Christ & paddle,
                     the petty moral

legalese peddled
         by people who try to shame
     my love for the flesh

                   of the world whose flesh
       I share :: that is why I walk
               out of everywhere ::

that is why I write
       this eighty miles from Philly ::
   it's sunny, humid

               even under oak
     & pine, the trail a rocky
             steep decline due east

between Hawk Mountain
      & Owl's Head :: I stop to rest
   then cross the River

                         of Rocks, a blockfield
              of boulders resulting from
                                        the cycle of freeze

& thaw at the edge
                of a glacier :: it's hard work
          to walk a mile in

                                        the uneven wake
                    of periglacial process
                                        whose sharp tilt hits shins

hardest, & harder
                to turn north on a trail aimed
          straight uphill & climb

                                        seven hundred feet
                    higher in less than a mile,
                                        a distance I feel

burn in my thighs, calves,
                & lungs, sweat sticking skin to
          shirt to pack :: I crest

                              at Kittatinny
                 Ridge, the trail shaded in part
                                    by young live hemlocks

white with adelgids,
              shed leaves an added padding
        on the Skyline Trail

                                   west to North Lookout ::
                   halfway, at East Rocks, the trees
                                    thin out to reveal

clear sky sans raptors
                    & I sit in the pale field
         of boulders, my feet

                                   a nest of nettles
                   whose sting I can neither touch
                                      nor escape :: the spurred

bones swell joints, afflict
                 skin with paresthesia, burn
         without remedy

                                        except to walk on,
                    let my mind vanish into
                                                    movement, suffering

that won't diminish
                    the fact that this form of life
            is my best, hillside

                                        below green & scarred
                    by dry skeletal hemlocks
                                                wrought in twists by wind,

my favorite part
                    the last climb up a cliffside
            capped by sandstone rocks

                                        where I sit & write ::
                    in October, just two months
                                                after the U. S.

bombs Japan, one month
                    after the war ends, Rachel
            Carson comes to watch

                              the fall migration
                    of raptors whose route follows
                                        Kittatinny Ridge

like a road :: in cold
                    wind on North Lookout she sits
            each day for two days

                                        until it begins
                        to rain :: she watches winged sky
                                        & thinks :: not of war,

nor of atomic
                    aftermath :: she sits, she thinks,
            on very old rock,

                                        & eras ago
                    creatures swim & die & drift
                                        to an ocean floor

slowing to sandstone
                    out of which uplift makes this
            mountain to which hawks

return :: I lie back
with half-closed eyes & try to
realize I am

at the bottom of
another ocean, she writes ::
the ocean of air

on which the hawks are
sailing :: when I return home
for a week I dream

we no longer leave
the cities :: we live downtown
high in posh office

buildings, in commons
linked by rope walkways, & grow
our food on the roofs ::

the dreams don't say why
the lower city's ruined,
unsafe for humans,

                                    but I know the streets
                    have grown thick with woods gray wolves
                                    hunt for white-tailed deer ::

at sunset we hear
                    coyotes yip on Broad Street,
        & later the wolves

                                    howl, echoing up
                    empty elevator shafts,
                                    city hall's stopped clock

a brooding yellow
                    gold round & wide as the eyes
        of the great horned owls

                                    who harrow field mice
                    they scare up in parking lots
                                    of cracked vast tarmac

lapsed into grassland
                    & bramble :: for seven nights
        I dream a city

of megafauna,
streets ruled by the dynamic
between prey species

& predators, scare
& chase, & for seven nights
I dream we all sleep

in a row of cots
lined up beneath a window
with a boardroom's view

of the powerless
city :: dreaming collective,
our job is to be

the afterimage
of history, of events
that pass before us

always new, always
identical :: no matter
that Carson appears

                                    before Congress in
                   June of 1963
                                                & asserts our right

to be secure in
                    our own homes against poisons
              applied by other

                                                persons :: no matter
                        that Section 27
                                                of Article 1

of Pennsylvania's
                        Constitution gives us all
                the right to clean air

                                                & water, & makes
                        these natural resources
                                                public, belonging

to the people :: no
                        matter that Teresa Hill
                protests the new plans

                                        to expand the site
                    of the refinery to
                                                other neighborhoods

& writes an open
                    letter to city council
            to remind them of

                                        chemistries unleashed
                    inside the bodies of all
                                                who live here :: through air

& water we know
                    industry already, know
            the toxicity

                                        of everyday life
                    measured in heavy metals
                                                & heightened immune

response, adrenal
                    fatigue, & microbiome
            imbalance :: my gut

a bloom of fungus,
my blood an arsenic sleeve,
a lead reservoir,

a wet rose loaded
with mercury, I walk out
into the city

that by all rights should
not be toxic :: no matter
whether my notebook

reads *spring* or *winter*,
whether the trees are in leaf
or bare, or whether

a man walks beside
me or I walk on alone,
the city differs

infinitely from
itself & remains, within
& without, always

                    already the same ::
          same derailed oil cars dangling
                              over the Schuylkill,

same worker hefting
                imported bouquets out of
        the back of his truck,

                                same asshole landlords
                    raising the rents, same subway
                                    graffiti saying

Philly is the B E S T
                M E S S, & it all resembles
        nothing so much as

                                late empire shaking
                    its waste stream into a blue
                                    metal maw that beeps

before it vomits
                its vast cache of trash into
        distant pits we pay

              to forget :: dreaming,
      the collective remembers
                  details, the crown vetch

blooming in a plot
        across the street from the struck
    doe made of paper

             & plastic, the sweet
       purple flowers on tendrils
              curling up from dirt

rutted by truck tread,
     a symbol of disturbed earth,
   the world a color

             trembling on its spine
      like the pages of a book
            whose intensity

I have to put down,
    its sentences persisting
  in the mind after,

so it's a Wednesday,
it's October 23rd,
it's 1940 ::

about five, I hear
for the first time the whistle
of bombs :: it's windy,

cloudy :: suddenly
I hear a plane :: suddenly
hear a whistle, see

smoke over the field
path :: then four separate thuds ::
& now it's March 5th,

2014,
a Wednesday, sparrows linger
on the windowsill,

& though it's wartime
we're no longer supposed to
feel it come so close,

                                we're not supposed to
                    notice that the chemicals
                                            we invent to help

us win the war through
                    which Woolf chooses not to live
            live on, dangerous

                                            in us :: & no one
                    hurt in the village, Woolf writes
                                            after the bombs land,

it's the cold hour, this,
                    before the lights go up :: snow-
            drops in the garden ::

                                            yes, I was thinking
                    we live without a future ::
                                            that's what's queer :: & now

to write, with a new
                    nib, & to go on wanting
            to catch the rhythm

                              of being open,
              critical, & also glad,
                                          married to the world

alive with the feel
                of mortal knowledge :: no high,
          no low, no great, no

                                    small :: no future full
              of forces that bind, connect,
                            & equal all ::

SITTING RIVER MEDITATION
(*Johnson, VT*)

At night the river,
        frozen over, fits

its bed like a key
        its lock. The current

keeps turning but
        the surface won't

open. I can
        hear ice click, shift,

its crystalline pins
        caught. Twenty miles south

of Lake Eden,
        its origin,

the Gihon's near its end.
        After the old red mill,

before it enters
        the Lamoille, it falls

flat, a closed
        door. Wrong key

in the wrong lock,
        I like to put

my mind where two worlds
        meet & agree to

disagree. The teachers
        say : take up the water,

make it your body
        & mind, make it thought.

But I think I
        must think the way

elements make
        temporary

arrangements
        with weather :

hydrogen locked
        to oxygen,

each strong molecule
        expands, a lattice

of tetrahedrons.
>All their new shapes make

ephemeral color
>the way what light there is

at midnight heightens
>ice, brighter briefly

than snow. & toward
>that whiteness my mind

pushes outward from
>the interior

where olivine water
>washes over gravel

& sand. Thought
>exerts drag

against the icy
>underside, & I

feel a border
>experience

can't cross over
>into knowledge

the way in front
        of paradox

my mind stops :
        for five years

my ill body killed me
        while it kept me alive.

On the bank bare
        brambles catch snow

weighted with rain
        that falls straight down,

hissing as it hits
        the ice. Who am I

now. Above : mountains.
        Below : the river.

Both moving & still,
        inaccessible

& everywhere, being
        is & keeps to itself,

hidden in emblems
        of the outward, seeds

extracted from bracts
        of a dry pine cone.

The spring equinox
        is near : rain coaxes

the icy lattices
        to relax into lapse,

little cracks
        mid-river.

It's so quiet
        I hardly feel

desire. But its soft force
        flenses the strongest water

from thaw : there, at
        the thinnest brink,

kinesis that
        resists stillness,

thinking on thinking,
        the current pulses.

CONVINCE ME YOU HAVE A SEED THERE
(*Johnson, VT*)

off Plot Road

in March thaw
I stop in a stand

of red pines

to listen to tilt
as each trunk

follows wind

in its crown
& sounds grain

against grain

straining noise
as intimate

as that of a joint

aching into age
I can see

outside the pines

the weave of things
crows in a lone oak

concatenating

the ecotone
where meadow

meets forest

white folks
clear cut

not long ago

to farm hay
on open land

later reclaimed

by the succession
of trees mostly

the mechanism

of small animals
& hard weather

on Clay Hill

above the valley
village I left

on foot to find

up Cemetery
Road the old

graves buried

in terraced drifts
headstones in rows

visible over snow

totally grayscale
except for sumac

at cemetery's edge

upright red
cones torching

holes in the visual

field the way
the fresh kill

I found en route

melted the snow
its startled predator

had dropped it in

blood & feathers
a deep wet nest

the day looked

less dense
without leaves

but winter felt

thicker with
the effort of getting

there & I went

on past graves
holding settlers

& Civil War vets

until the pines
seemed to charm

me out of myself

to stop & stand
& think touching

their live hard sides

of Plato's vision
the human not

an earthly but

a heavenly plant
the soul housed

in the head

threaded down
out of abstract

heaven to live

in the physical
soil the human

rooted in the two

worlds I look
up to see

each trunk

unsettled by wind
torque makes

groan & crowns

twist against
roots in earth

the way I might

fight an idea
that seizes me

with its weather

& I wonder
what it sounds like

the loblolly

bioengineered
by ArborGen®

its genes spliced

with Monterey pine
mouse ear cress

sweet gum

& even e. coli
to become

disease resistant

a SuperTree™
what makes a tree

their website asks

valuable & answers
superior growth

maximum value

approved by feds
its dense straight

grained wood

climbs to forty six
feet over nine

growing seasons

each tree a version
of Plato's vision

an earthly plant

imbued with *eidos*
enough to better

bring it to market

the heavenly power
that keeps the tree

reaching toward it

a cold winter's
warm day

filled the walk

uphill with thaw
falling loud

from eaves & limbs

& rills thrilled
the angled road

my socks are wet

& I stand thinking
of Thoreau who wrote

convince me you have

a seed there
& I am prepared

to expect wonders

& I think
of transgenic pollen

germinating

after it travels
hundreds of miles

& how farmers

can't contain
cross-pollination

between spliced

& wild species
& how hybrid trees

will intertwine

with the hungers
of the red squirrel

paused sideways

bright against
dark bark

an acorn between

its orange teeth
& I do not move

further toward

the laboratory
future sewn

in genes chosen

& fused to produce
fruit & fall

to seed a kind

of life not yet
legible to us

I want to believe

wind will make
new wood grain

groan & yellow

curtains of pollen
will billow after

mud season

finishes off
a long winter

I want to believe

birds will drop
coniferous seeds

in fields cleared

of old red oak
& rodents will store

hoards of acorns

that will root
& rise after fires

clear out dry pines

& all will continue
the succession

of trees in a world

in which we'll touch
others invented

for a profit made

ontological
the very genome

grafted to capital

I stand inside
the charm the stand

makes out of wind

the stand someone
planted & didn't

harm or harvest

& so has persisted
beyond human

use for so long

the base of each
trunk is ringed

thick with moss

watered by runoff
washing nutrients

down yards of bark

years of touch
create this color

collaring the pines

with a green brighter
than their needles

material relation

the ensoiled soul
we're rooted in

the way *heaven*

derives itself
from words for *sky*

& words for *stone*

the way a birch
has infiltrated

the symmetrical

stand at an angle
weighted by snow

its rough trunk

bent & its bark
sloughing off

botched swaths

around lichen
in wide ruptures

working upward

a sort of saffron
stain the startle

of fox piss in snow

OLIVINE, QUARTZ, GRANITE, CARNELIAN
(*Johnson, VT*)

On foot under thunder
        heading in from the west,
I wasn't thinking *rain*

        but now I'm thinking *rain*
on Plot Road while I watch
        Foote Brook do its thaw thing :

ropy cold clear water
        pulls itself downhill fast,
its spatter lathering

        granite banks with foam. Up-
hill, up the road, a field
        mown gold. Its curve is cut

by horizon, a veil
        of rain drawn across it
slowly so it darkens

in increments. I left
the house without poncho
or umbrella. I'm cold.

The good news is : the way
Archimedes wanted
a place to stand to lift

the world, & Descartes sought
one thought as certain as
the point a lever turns

into a fulcrum, this
dirt road is a fine place
to get totally soaked

in the poem. The bad
news is : el niño. It's
a bummer to go all

cogito here after
the hottest winter in
the hottest year so far

on record, all the thaw
finished by the first week
of March. Yet I can feel

the color the poem
gathers inside me, brown
silver interior

of a dried milkweed pod,
everything outside it
on a spectrum of wet

& getting wetter as
the front moves overhead.
A little mist sizzles

high in the canopy,
its sound in the middle
distance of the sonic

landscape between Foote Brook
& thunder, a distance
rusty blackbirds also

fill from the oak they have
flocked to, so raucously
          dominating its crown.

When the rain hits, they fall
          silent. Then there's nothing
in the hush but thunder

          & water on water
& water hitting wood.
          Above : the sky a kind

of crushed lilac. Around
          me : Clay Hill an issue
of trickles gathering

          gravity gathering
mass heading south downhill
          to the river. Little

streams even in the mud
          under my feet, I want
to say I feel the pull

        on all my vertebrae,
occiput to sacrum,
        the water in my bones

longing to join the thaw.
        & thought alluvial
too, the way valleys fill

        slowly with gravel sent
down by the surrounding
        mountains : olivine, quartz,

granite, carnelian,
        each stone an idea
washed then carried by rain.

        Down Foote Brook's leaf-slick steep
bank I slide the way *walk*
        & *watch* begin in rhyme

then fail the way those same
        activities fit in-
side each other until

they don't : I slip, hit rock,
my body stops, the walk
        stalls, & I sit, my mind

rising toward quiet
        as the brook goes by, south
by southwest. I watch, let

        the current take over.
Over its rocky bed
        the water runs clear, leaves

the distortions made by
        its torsion flickering
the way musculature

        moves its skin, all flexure
& shadow. *Do not move*
        the x-ray tech told me,

so I stood & did what
        I'm doing now : I watched
living turn to image,

a bruised sort of bluish
fluid on a white screen
        the rheumatologist

lit up. *You might have years
        of mobility left*
if *you're careful*, he said.

        I could've looked like that
for hours at my spine,
        the molecules locked in

degrading matrices :
        where the joints meet up, spurs
curve small bone hooks honed to

        catch on flesh the x-rays
see through, causing the doc
        to write in his report,

*soft tissues unremark-
        able*. It's weird to be
always incurring off-

        screen injuries I have
to live with. The process
        makes a space in my thought

like I make a space on
        the brook's hard bank : anthro-
pogenic nonpoint source

        pollutant, my urine
a potent effluent
        of medicines I need

& pesticides I don't,
        a pharmacopeia
of harm for riverine

        species. I close my eyes.
Rain on leaf litter sounds
        like storm wind high above

& the brook thrown downhill
        by its own force, the world
coalescing briefly

        in an unending rhyme
with itself, consonant
        & comforting. I know

it's cogito that makes
        it seem my ears make it
so. I open my eyes.

        I get up & go east,
back up Plot Road, muddy
        now with runoff. Off-road

landscape ranges from field
        to forest to dwelling
& back, the visual

        rhythm of settlement
& regrowth, clearcutting
        & aftermath, my eye

always drawn to eco-
        tone, richly liminal
& ugly where forest

meets field grown over stumps.
I love what yields green there
        then dries in thickets : bull

thistle, milkweed, seedheads
        in hundreds that luster
against the denser screen

        of trees. I love how birds
the size of sparrows hunt
        in the scrub, break cover

to duck between thin trunks –
        the black-capped chickadee
loosing its slow two-note

        sing-song sing-song only
after it lands a branch.
        Some things must be listened

into appearances :
        the thistles for instance
rustle, sigh into sight,

vatic static in wave
patterns that predict wind
             that hits my face; the rain

insinuates itself
             slowly into puddles
of an abalone

             silver, iridescent
as a rock pigeon's neck;
             & the poem starts first

as a color I hear,
             its stiff dry stalks shaking
gray & brown. It's almost

             pornographic, detail
the world offers, texture
             whose totality is

far beyond adequate
             capture, & excites me
anyway, as endless

as the filaments of
beard lichen the same soft
        bright green of olivine.

So I watch; I walk on;
        I fill my pockets full
of milkweed pods, a few

        still stuffed with floss; I watch
as if I could forget
        the harm that happens where

the world's flesh meets my flesh;
        I walk as if I could
undo the human self

        I've become & remain
through undoing done to
        others. Between *walking*

& *watching* the whole world
        slips, goes missing, my mind
empty as the chambers

of a gun whose bullets
have hit the intended
targets, residual

heat & soft black powder
all that cogito leaves
behind. I never meant

to fire. It's not my voice
that cries out *bulls-eye!* but
I find my mouth moves too

without thinking as each
species goes down. & then
I do nothing but think,

for instance, of a cave
in upstate New York : there
a fungus introduced

from Europe infected
bats whose skin spread through touch
a syndrome inducing

          the inability
to hibernate. Awake,
        sick bats use up winter

fat stores & starve, thinned wings
         torn, riddled with lesions.
As hibernacula

        emptied in the east, spores
moved mortality cross-
        country to thirty three

states in the mere decade
        since the fungus first jumped
the Atlantic on some

        spelunker's boots, perhaps,
or on infected gear –
        extinction follows us

whether we mean it to
        or not. *We* are the point
the lever turns into

a fulcrum : by wounding
the world we lift ourselves
            up. So I walk the way

enthusiasm means
            I'm possessed by some god –
I don't know how to know

            what I know except to
put it on foot, gesture
            as outwardly useless

as boots in a downpour
            on a scale this total.
Just before Plot Road meets

            Clay Hill, an abandoned
barn leans over a stream
            that cuts under its right

back corner, its skewed floor
            strewn still with tools & hay.
A few license plates hang

on its aged gray façade.
I like the look of it
the way I like the sound

of the passing cars harped
on Clay Hill by frost heaves
that rattle their chassis :

laughable enchantment,
the sort of ruin
that seems livable

until it isn't.

SITTING ISOHYDRIC MEDITATION

weather is water
      is one way to think

about the season
      seizing the street tree

another drought year
      measured in questions

I asked the nurses
      who gently strapped me

to the clang & throb
      inside the passing

time the MRI
      ground into windows

the doctor looked through
      to see my future

I sit on the couch
      & watch the sparrows

on the branches pant
     & puff their feathers

a sort of solstice
     truce with the dry heat

moving scorch from edge
     to stem on each leaf

the heat's so quiet
     it's a kind of pain

nothing seems to soothe
     not even his damp

armpit & its scent
     of moss soaked with rain

woody sweet dear
     bacterial earth

mouth my mouth opens
     onto & into

his skin confusing
     outside inside me

when we fuck we go
     deep mammal all fur

& genital scent
        in my beard a soak

of pheromones taut
        swollen erectile

tissue & the swoon
        of adrenaline

a chemical world
        that feels insular

but is immersed in
        stimulus the way

a magnetic field
        held my prone body

whose protons aligned
        their axes & flipped

their spins to allow
        radio waves

through flesh made newly
        resonant I felt

removed from the world
        & cocooned in sound

while the protons slowed
      & their spins flipped back

radio signals
      that rendered image

vertebral detail
      so precise it hurt

to look at the bones
      as the doctor talked

drought's about being
      porous & storing

water if you can't
      travel to get it

so some tree species
      close their stomata

& wait for water
      the way maples do

dying slowly from
      edges to center

as a stress response
      it's a real gamble

to shut yourself up
        inside of yourself

if I could I would
        stay as open as

his face when I sit
        on his cock & he

holds my hips & tilts
        himself up deeper

injury insists
        it remain hidden

& grows its quota
        of pain from the bones

the doctor showed me
        calcifications

white as dry lichen
        leaching life from

a lip of granite
        how to keep going

into the quotient
        of future the bones

divide inside me
      the incurable

instance a given
      faultless or at fault

I remain hidden
      how to keep going

DOOMSTEAD DAYS

today's gender is rain

it touches everything

with its little silver

epistemology

mottled like a brook trout

with a hundred spots

white as bark scars

on this slim trunk

thrust up from

one sidewalk square

the four square feet

of open ground

given a street tree

twiggy perimeter

continually clipped

by parking or car door

or passing trash truck

that snaps an actual

branch I find haunting

the little plot

its winged achenes

auto-rotate down to

it's not that I don't

like a wide sidewalk

or the 45 bus

that grinds right by

but if organisms

didn't insist on

forms of resistance

they'd be dead

of anthropocentric

technomechanical

systems whose grids

restrict the living

through perpetual stress

that elicits intense

physical response

like an animal

panic hitting

the psoas with cramps

or root fungus sunk in

the maple's allotment

of city property

as tolerably wide

as the migraine

that begins at the base

of my skull & pinches

with breadth calipers

my temples until

the feel of flay arrays

the dura's surface

inside the bones inside

the head the healer holds

in her hands & says

the occiput is shut

flat & irks the nerves

that thread through its

unappeasable shunt

into the spine I see

a white light I keep

thinking about the way

long drought dries out

topsoil so deep beneath

its surface the first

hard rain wreaks flood

taking the good dirt

with it the way today's

wet excess escapes

its four square feet

of exposed root

& rivers out

a flex of sediment

alluvial over

the civic cement

of the anthropocene

in currents a supple

rippled velvet dun

as Wissahickon Creek

in fall's brief season

of redd & spawn

when brook trout

in chill quick shallows

once dug into gravel

to let nested eggs

mix with milt

& turn pearls

translucent as raw

unpolished quartz

each white-eyed ova

flawed by a black fleck

my eyes close over

at the height of migraine

fertile error waiting

with incipient tail

ready to propel it

deeper into nausea

until the healer halts

its hatching & calms

neuralgia between

the heels of her hands

pressing the occiput

back open into

the natural curve

the bones forget

the way the banks

of the Wissahickon

have forgotten rapids

rinsing schist shaded

by hemlock that kept

the brook trout cold

each patterned aspect

of habitat lost

first to dams & mills

& industry runoff

& plots of flax

Germantown planted

for paper & cloth

made with water's power

& hauled out of

the precipitous gorge

up rough narrow roads

south to the city port

before adelgids

took the crucial dark

from under hemlocks

sun heating the rocky

creek down steep rills

to the lower Schuylkill

wide in its final miles

dammed at Fairmount

for two centuries

of coal silt & dredge

fabric dye & sewage

that gave rise to typhus

& refinery spills

that gave rise to fire

rinsed by this gender

that remembers

current's circuit

anadromous shad

& striped bass

leaving the Atlantic

heading upriver

shedding saltwater

for fresh in runs

whose numbers turned

the green river silver

if color counts as

epistemology

spring sun on the backs

of a thousand shad

is a form of knowing

local to another

century & the duller

color of ours

is the way the word

gender remembers

it once meant to fuck

beget or give birth

sibling to *generate*

& *engender* all

fertile at the root

& continuous

as falling water

molecules smoothing

the sparkling gnarl

of Wissahickon schist

until its surface

mirrors their force

the fuel element

& fundament alike

derive thriving from

being at its biggest

when it's kinetic

energy headed

toward intensity

everything's body

connected by this

totally elastic

materiality

I feel as ecstatic

wide dilation

when the shut skull

gives up resistance

to the healer's hands

& the occiput

opens its bones

my mind's eye goes

OKAY I'm awake now

rowdy with trout

psoas relaxed

my body's a conduit

it roars with water

passing from past

to present through

pipes & riparian

ecotones alike

all of my fluids

pollutants cycling

back into my own

watershed toxins

& heavy metals

bonded to blood

stored in liver & fat

C8 glyphosate

mercury & lead

it's awkward okay

I keep thinking about

the man who asks me

to visit his doomstead

which seems kinky

for a first date

what's the safeword

for men with genders

built for the world's end

men with weaponized

genders hoarding solar

power & canned goods

bottled water genders

tending small vegetable

gardens out back

behind the chickens

concrete genders sealed

in lead their doors

secured from inside

with thick steel bars

fringe libertarian

endtimes genders

hetero girlie

camo gun calendars

apocalyptic tits

pinned on brick walls

by lone bunks

so the men can cross out

each day once

civil society

ends with a pathetic

snivel like *please help*

doomstead men live

doomstead days already

sealed in extreme fiction

as if there were

ever a way to stay

safely self-contained

by which I mean

the anthropocene

is its own gender

biospheric in scale

its persistent flux

from fossil record

to Antarctic ice core

so uncontainable

we all exhibit it

with a local sense

of personal chosen

expression strategic

or contingent

like fertility

medicalized tracked

managed or casual

happy fucking

without a condom

risky given the odds

leveraged against us

& the blameless

microbes seeking

homes in our nooks

& tubes so I don't

visit his doomstead

a psychic structure

I feel in my head

as blocked thought

I watch play out

in the Schuylkill

where it pools wide

shallow with silt

above Fairmount dam

I stand on the bank

& know I'm not

supposed to posit

an analogy

between the river

& my body but

courtesy of this dam

the city siphons

its water into me

another human

intervention

diverting its path

each of my cells

a little prison

the river sits in

so we're related

on a molecular

level so intimate

I think I can say

it wants speed

& movement free

enough to jump

the strained relation

to human needs

it serves without relief

without the hands

that hold my bones

& tend my fascia

that remember

a different posture

without blockage

or pain a model

for undoing harm

done by capital

empowered to frack

during record drought

millions of gallons

of toxic wastewater

injected into earth

or kept in open ponds

prone & porous

in western counties

where river otters

have rebounded after

last being spotted

in the Allegheny

in 1899

otters are raucous

& chirp chitter

chuckle & grumble

when wrestling together

or sliding on ice

playful biophony

rivers have missed

for a whole century

like brook trout rooting

in loose cool gravel

or the plash of insects

fallen from hemlocks

the intact eastern

riverine biome

one serious mess

of sound enmeshed

in sound enmeshed

in biotic patterns

as heavy as traffic

when the weekend

weather is nice

& I ride the early

27 bus

to the Wissahickon

it's not that I don't like

the city it's just if

biodiversity

is a measure of health

a city is

by definition sick

with people & built

structures crowding

out other lives

though I love signs

species persist

this sidewalk moss

probably *bryum*

argentum native

to guano-covered

seabird rookeries

this fertile gingko

stinking up the street

with stone fruits

crushed underfoot

this nameless fern

in a downpipe drain

so modest in scale

like the simple songs

of house sparrows

everywhere though

this chubby one

is hustling a fallen

everything bagel

of seeds & crumbs

& it's not that I don't

like people either

our sociality

genitals & smells

interesting diction

surprising privacies

revealed at parties

bars & in bedrooms

our genders in acts

various & wet

as thought product

of dissolved salts

washing our brains

in rich cognition

that falters without

water which can't be

taken by the head

in the hands & held

in the hopes of healing

its body is too vast

its mind boundless

by definition

the world is awake

be careful my dears

it is the gender

that remembers

everything

ACKNOWLEDGMENTS

Thank you to the following organizations for crucial support that made the writing of this book possible: the Pew Center for Arts & Heritage, the Headlands Center for the Arts, the Vermont Studio Center, the MacDowell Colony, the Fund for Poetry & Temple University.

  ::

Thank you to Tyler Meier & Hannah Ensor of the University of Arizona Poetry Center for the invitation to participate in their 2016-17 Poetry + Climate Change series. That invitation sparked the research & hikes that generated "Doomstead Days." Jared Stanley's *Ears* suggested the form the poem took. & Dr. Meghna Shah released the poem.

  ::

Thank you to the following publications & their editors for publishing poems (sometimes in earlier versions):

American Poet: selections from "Headlands Quadrats"
Blackbird: selections from "Headlands Quadrats"
Kenyon Review: "Clear Water Renga"
      & "Convince me you have a seed there"
KROnline: "Olivine, Quartz, Granite, Carnelian"
New England Review: "Sitting Isohydric Meditation"
       & "Sitting River Meditation" (as "After a Long Illness")
Oversound: "Doomstead Days"
VOLT: "Toxics Release Inventory"

  ::

Thank you to MC Hyland, Anna Gurton-Wachter & Jeff Peterson of DoubleCross Press for the beautiful chapbook version of *Headlands Quadrats*.

::

Thank you to Rick Barot, Gillian Conoley & Jared Stanley for the thorough read-throughs of the book & to David Baker, Jericho Brown, Allison Cobb, Sue Landers & Susan Tichy for reading & commenting on parts of it in manuscript.

::

& thank you especially to Stephen Motika, Lindsey Boldt, Andrea Abi-Karam, Janet Evans-Scanlon & all the staff at Nightboat.

BRIAN TEARE is the author of six critically acclaimed books, most recently *Companion Grasses*, which was a finalist for the Kingsley Tufts Award, *The Empty Form Goes All the Way to Heaven*, and *Doomstead Days*, longlisted for the National Book Award and a finalist for the National Book Critics Circle and Kingsley Tufts Awards. His honors include the Brittingham Prize and Lambda Literary and Publishing Triangle Awards, as well as fellowships from the NEA, the Pew Foundation, the American Antiquarian Society, the Headlands Center for the Arts, and the MacDowell Colony. After over a decade of teaching and writing in the San Francisco Bay Area, and eight years in Philadelphia, he's now an Associate Professor at the University of Virginia, and lives in Charlottesville, where he makes books by hand for his micropress, Albion Books.

NIGHTBOAT BOOKS

Nightboat Books, a nonprofit organization, seeks to develop audiences for writers whose work resists convention and transcends boundaries. We publish books rich with poignancy, intelligence, and risk. Please visit our website, www.nightboat.org, to learn about our titles and how you can support our future publications.

The following individuals have supported the publication of this book. We thank them for their generosity and commitment to the mission of Nightboat Books:

Kazim Ali
Anonymous
Photios Giovanis
Elenor & Thomas Kovachevich
Elizabeth Motika
Leslie Scalapino – O Books Fund
Benjamin Taylor
Jerrie Whitfield & Richard Motika

In addition, this book has been made possible, in part, by grants from the National Endowment for the Arts and the New York State Council on the Arts Literature Program.